Main Streets of Southeast Asia

MAIN STREETS OF SOUTHEAST ASIA

TEXT AND PHOTOGRAPHS BY

Hal Buell

DODD, MEAD & COMPANY

New York

For Angela

Picture Credits:
Alan Cline—page 72
Indonesian embassy, Tokyo—page 105
Pacific Area Travel Association—pages 102, 103, 109
Keystone, British picture agency—pages 101, 104, 106,
107, 108, 110, 111

Contents

Main Streets of Southeast Asia

A LOOK AT
SOUTHEAST ASIA

A Chinese junk, its massive, ribbed sails full to the wind, passes a huge, diesel-powered freighter in the calm waters between the Chinese mainland and the crowded island of Hong Kong. Overhead a jet airliner glides gracefully to a landing on an airstrip that juts into the harbor. Passengers peering from the windows feel as though they can reach out and touch the countless wooden junks that house refugee families from Communist China and families of fishermen that work the South China Sea.

This scene of striking contrasts in Hong Kong is typical of Southeast Asia—where the modern world and ancient Oriental tradition meet and attempt to find common ground.

In Jakarta, capital of the island nation of Indonesia, a wrinkle-faced Moslem stands in a shimmering, white mosque and sings evening praises to Allah. Only a few miles away a jet fighter touches down after a training flight. Still farther away, in Bali,

7

Hindus participate in religious dances as old as the religion itself.

In Manila, capital of The Philippines, a high-wheeled *calisa,* pulled by a pony, competes for space with a huge delivery truck in an American-style traffic jam.

In the jungles outside Saigon, barefoot village militiamen, some armed with the latest automatic weapons, join comrades armed with makeshift spears to fight off night raids of marauders.

A Meo tribesman in Laos, his silver necklace sparkling in the mountain sunshine, listens to a transistor radio made in Japan.

In Cambodia's capital of Phnom Penh swingy western dance music at a French-style cafe blends with the tinkly sounds accompanying a dance rehearsal at the Royal Palace.

A Thai boatman, on his way to Bangkok's market place on the canals, gently guides his vessel past a modern night club and an air-conditioned theatre showing the latest European and American films.

Just a few miles outside these cities, however, this world of contrast ends and much of old Asia remains. Bandits loot and pillage, starvation takes its yearly toll, rumbling volcanoes spread their destruction, floods wash away the rice crop, disease infects the young and old, sapping the energy of these young nations.

This is Southeast Asia, a gigantic combination of mainland nations and island countries, largely jungle-land, always hot and humid and tropical, often populated by elephants and tigers, but spotted here and there with huge modern cities.

Southeast Asia is generally considered the area west from The Philippines and east from Burma; south from the border of China and north from the Indonesian islands.

On the map the area looks somewhat like an extra piece of land stuck on the side of India and China, fringed with an island necklace and possessing a long, narrow piece of land, or peninsula, on the left.

The nations and possessions are: Hong Kong, The Philippines,

Thailand, Laos, Cambodia, Viet Nam, Burma, Malaya, Singapore and Indonesia.

Indonesia is by far the largest country, with ninety million people and 736,000 square miles of land in the many islands that make up the archipelago. The tiny city-state of Singapore is the smallest —fewer than two million people living on 217 square miles of land.

All but one of these nations—Thailand—have been ruled by a major Western power. In some cases it was an oppressive rule and hence, today, new-found freedoms have instilled in the hearts and minds of most Southeast Asians a passionate desire to avoid any future course which could return dictatorial rule by a foreign power.

The 207 million people of Southeast Asia are a vast mixture. Their religions, for example, are typical of this great melting pot. The Philippines, thousands of miles from Rome, are 90 per cent Roman Catholic. But their island neighbors—the Indonesians— make up the greatest Moslem nation on earth, likewise thousands of miles from the mother country of Arabia. Buddhism, brought in from India, predominates on the Southeast Asian mainland.

The people themselves are white, black, brown and yellow. They speak many languages—the old colonial tongues of French, English, and Dutch; the new national languages that seek to unite the various regions of many countries; and countless dialects that sometimes obstruct progress toward national unity.

This mixture is a direct result of Southeast Asia's geographical position. Look at a map of the world and you will see that this area is located around the South China Sea and astride the great trade routes that centuries ago linked India and China with the Western world. In fact, it was only by accident that America was discovered as European traders looked for a short cut to this fabulously wealthy and interesting part of the world.

But that is getting ahead of our story.

In ancient times China, then an immensely powerful nation, received tribute from many of the small kingdoms of Southeast Asia. Even before the birth of Christ the Chinese were traveling into Southeast Asia, usually on military expeditions. Because of China's great power her influence was easily established. Many of these small kingdoms have disappeared. But every once in a while the remains of an old palace, covered by trees and vines of the jungle and lived in by tigers and elephants, is discovered.

About 2,000 years ago Indian merchants came to Southeast Asia. With them came Buddhism and Hinduism, and their written language called Sanskrit.

Approximately the same time, the first Arabs came to Southeast Asia by sea from the Middle East. Seeking the rich spices that fetched high prices in the bazaars of Baghdad and Cairo, and in European nations as well, the Arabs traded in the Indonesian islands and up and down the Malay peninsula. This is how Indonesia got its old name of "Spice Islands."

The Arabs brought with them their religion—Islam, whose followers are called Moslems—and to this day magnificent mosques, as beautiful as those in the Middle East, are found in Indonesia and Malaya.

Naturally, when the Arabs sold their spices—things like nutmeg and cinnamon and pepper—in western markets, European traders started sending their own ships to Southeast Asia.

And so the Westerners came to the South China Sea.

This was mostly in the 17th and 18th centuries—fabulous days when pirates and sultans alike preyed on the fantastically wealthy European galleons bearing their riches to the markets of Spain, England, Holland, France and Portugal.

The sultans of Southeast Asia, however, fought among themselves, too. Soon some sultans formed alliances with western nations against other sultans. The result was that the Westerners soon controlled virtually all of the South China Sea area. Only Thailand remained free.

The British were especially strong in Malaya and Burma and often fought with the Dutch, who controlled the Indonesian islands. The French ruled Indo-China, now known as Cambodia, Laos and Viet Nam. The Spanish ruled The Philippines until 1898 when the islands went to the United States after the Spanish-American War.

During World War II invading Japanese armies conquered the area in surprisingly quick time. But their rule was short-lived. An Allied victory in 1945 returned the Japanese conquerors to their home islands. Western powers returned to claim their former possessions.

But the situation had changed. The people of Southeast Asia wanted independence. And they were willing to fight for it. Many did. Soon all the countries—save a few scattered possessions—were free.

Now, let's look at these countries as they are today.

HONG KONG

Where East and West Meet

When Hong Kong became a colony of England in 1841 there were only a few Chinese fishermen living there. They fished the waters of the South China Sea in great wooden junks, or sailing vessels.

Today, junks much like those built more than 100 years ago are still seen in Hong Kong's beautiful harbor. But in place of the few tiny fishing villages there now stands a great trading center with a population of more than three million persons. It is one of the world's most fascinating cities and is generally considered a good example of the harmonious blending of Eastern and Western cultures.

Ocean liners and jet planes daily bring a continuous flow of tourists and goods to Hong Kong. Prices are good in Hong Kong because it is a free port—that is, the government permits most items to enter the English colony duty-free. And tourists have a shopping holiday buying the latest manufactured items from

12

Japan, Europe and the United States, or beautiful silks and art objects from India and the other nations of Southeast Asia.

Most of the people and a great portion of the businesses are found on Hong Kong island. A ferry-boat—much like the ferries used in New York City or San Francisco—links the island with the Hong Kong mainland which is called Kowloon.

Hong Kong island is an exciting mixture of London and Shanghai. Double-decked trolleys travel through the streets of Victoria, Hong Kong's main city. Chinese businessmen ride in rickshaws, open carriages on two wheels which are pulled by a man.

Great brownstone office buildings built fifty years ago and multi-storied, glass-walled banks line the main streets, suggestive of New York City's Wall Street and London's Fleet Street. But around the corner, up the side streets, old China takes over. Cooked ducks hang in shop windows, one-man restaurants serve a quick bowl of rice to laborers, countless metal items hanging out for sale in the Chinese hardware stores clatter in the wind. And overhead, from the windows of crowded tenements, wash is put out to dry on endless thousands of bamboo poles.

Hong Kong's British atmosphere is the result of the long rule of the island by a colonial government. The island was awarded to the British in 1841 after a war with China. The area called Kowloon, on the Chinese mainland, was given to England after another war in 1860. Additional land was acquired by England in 1898 under a leasing arrangement with China. This extra area was called the New Territories. Altogether, Hong Kong today is 400 square miles in size.

Because it is so small, there is not sufficient space for the millions of people that live there. Since 1949, when Communist forces conquered the China mainland, refugees have flocked to Hong Kong. They have even built shacks on the sides of the rocky hills overlooking Victoria. During the typhoon season violent rainstorms wash some of these shacks away, often killing many people.

13

The crowded conditions have forced many of the people to live on the water in junks or smaller Chinese boats called sampans. There are several places in Hong Kong where hundreds of these boats are lashed together, with boardwalks between them for sidewalks. These boats are never used for transportation—just for housing.

Travelers in Southeast Asia generally agree that this British Crown Colony where East and West meet is one of the area's most interesting cities.

The Star Ferry churns across Hong Kong harbor from Kowloon on the mainland to Victoria, the main city on Hong Kong island. This harbor is one of the most beautiful in the world—and also one of the busiest. Old wooden junks ferrying goods from freighters to shore, or returning from fishing runs on the open sea, glide across the calm waters. Small sampans, warships of the U. S. Navy, and the sleek, private yachts of wealthy Chinese and European businessmen are moored in the harbor. The city seen in the background of this picture is Victoria.

A walk through the streets of Victoria, on Hong Kong island, can be a fascinating stroll. There are the old British-style office buildings, like these, which house famous business firms operating in Asia. Along this street, as on many thoroughfares in Hong Kong, a double-decker tram carries passengers to and from work. Hong Kong is the only city in Asia that has such double-deck trolleys.

Hong Kong also has modern, glass-walled office buildings, just like those in New York City. The difference is that at any time you might see a rickshaw man, with his ancient means of transportation, waiting for a customer on a busy boulevard.

But most of Hong Kong is Chinese—crowded, filled with countless stores and stalls selling an endless variety of goods, from pens to cooked ducks. From many of the main streets stone steps carry the shopper up Hong Kong's hilly side streets, deeper and deeper into the Chinese way of life . . .

. . . until finally the western influence has disappeared entirely and scenes as old as China itself greet the eye. A laborer carries his load attached to both ends of a pole, balanced on his shoulder. Overhead, washing hangs out on bamboo poles to catch a bit of sunlight that never quite seems to find its way to street level in these crowded sections of Hong Kong.

A workman carries his load on a street in Hong Kong.

An elderly Chinese gentleman watches the activity on the street in front of his house.

20

For sheer physical beauty it is hard to find a place in Southeast Asia that compares with Hong Kong. Its coastline is marked by beautiful small bays, with steep cliffs on each side reaching down to the water.

Some of these harbors provide a shelter from ocean winds and storm for the many thousands of families that live on sampans and junks. Opposite, a mother, carrying her child on her back, paddles out to do some shopping on shore.

Life aboard a sampan can be cold in Hong Kong's winter season—it is the only Southeast Asian country that is not hot the year around—but usually these families have much more room than they would have living in the city.

One of Hong Kong's biggest tourist attractions is Tiger Balm Garden. Built by the maker of a patent medicine as a memorial, the garden is dominated by a great, white pagoda that can be seen from many places in Victoria. Children delight in the brightly colored cement reproductions of characters from Chinese stories, and in the special scenes created just for the garden.

THAILAND

Heart of Southeast Asia

If you look at a map of Southeast Asia you will see one country right in the middle that looks like the head of an elephant. It seems to have big, fan-like ears and a head with a trunk dangling down one side of the Malayan peninsula.

The country is Thailand—once called Siam. Its capital is Bangkok, one of Southeast Asia's most colorful cities.

Visitors to this city of one million persons usually remember two things above all others—Bangkok's magnificent temples and palaces and its countless *klongs*, or canals.

The temples and palaces give Bangkok a storybook atmosphere —golden spires as high as eight stories, multi-colored buildings, great stone giants twenty-feet high standing guard at palace gates, and thousands of Buddhist monks, their heads shaved, wearing saffron yellow robes.

To step into these palaces and temples is to step back two centuries into history when powerful kings ruled Thailand—far-

25

sighted kings who were quick to adopt modern ways and pave the way for Thailand's advancement. There was a famous book, play and movie written about one of these kings and his English school teacher called *Anna and the King of Siam*.

Bangkok's other interesting feature, its *klongs*, has resulted in a nickname for the city—Venice of the Orient. Like that fabulous city of Europe, Bangkok has a great network of canals. At one time there were very few roads in the city and people traveled entirely on these canals. Even today many people use them. Women, wearing huge straw hats that look exactly like lampshades, take coconuts and other tropical fruits to the market place on the *klongs*. Many people live on the canals, in houses built on stilts over the water. Thai children have a wonderful time hanging onto ropes trailing behind boats which pull them through the water.

But like practically all Southeast Asian capitals, Bangkok has a modern side, too. Next to the *klongs* are modern highways, and it is a common sight to see limousines whisk over a bridge as a country woman guides her flat boat on the water below.

There are air-conditioned movies that show the latest American and European films. There are wide boulevards jammed with traffic, and imposing buildings that house the government offices of this land of twenty million people.

Many homes have television sets—even some of those built high on stilts above the *klong* water. And in the morning, modern, motor-driven boats cruise down the *klongs* picking up students to take them to school.

The Thais have been very fortunate. Thanks to the hot, humid climate of the country and the lack of mountains, there has always been abundant rice.

There is one other important thing to know about Thailand. Although every other nation in Southeast Asia has been ruled by a Western power, Thailand somehow managed to remain free. Because of her strategic geographical position, she acted as a buffer state between various colonial powers. And her kings, besides being far-sighted, were also clever politicians.

Hence, today Thailand stands as one of Southeast Asia's most stable, advanced and prosperous nations, headquarters of the Southeast Asia Treaty Organization (SEATO) and a member of the United Nations.

Although the Thais dearly love their King and Queen, political power is in the hands of a Prime Minister.

Most of the people who live in Thailand are Buddhists, like this woman who rolls a prayer stone forward and backward before a small image of Buddha. Many Southeast Asians are Buddhists, but in few places has this religion inspired monuments as spectacular as those in Bangkok. This scene is on the grounds of the Temple of the Emerald Buddha. Huge stone giants, called *yeaks*, stand guard at the entrance to the city's Grand Palace. The spiraling pagoda in the background is golden.

School boys watch a monk feed pigeons at a Bangkok *wat*, which is what the Thais call a temple. Before they reach manhood most of these lads will spend some time living in a *wat*, learning about Buddhism. They will have all their hair shaved off and they will wear saffron colored robes . . .

30

. . . like this young monk who confers with an elder. They are seated before a typical altar, shrouded in darkness, with a black, seated Buddha in the background.

A group of Thai high school boys have their art class at Wat Ben-jamabophit, better known as the Marble Temple. This structure, made largely of Italian marble, is one of the most magnificent places of worship in all of Southeast Asia.

A favorite game of Thai school boys is to stand in a circle and kick a straw ball back and forth, as these youngsters do during recess period in Bangkok. Most school boys in Thailand wear brown shorts and white shirts like those worn by these boys. A typical Bangkok schoolhouse is in the background.

Like all world capitals, Bangkok has many traffic-filled streets and boulevards. But the Thai capital has streets of water, too—the *klongs*. Each day they are jammed with countless boats, water taxis and swimmers. Boatmen-merchants sell everything from coconuts to cold drinks, from fancy shirts to hardware.

Many Thais live on the *klongs* in houses like these, complete with modern refrigerators and television sets. From their homes inches above the water . . .

. . . the Thais travel about Bangkok on their errands. Or go to school by water taxi, like these school children.

Bangkok is one of the few Southeast Asian capitals that has a trolley system. Because Thailand is always warm, the trolleys do not have doors or windows and the driver handles the controls in the open air. The sign on the front of the trolley is written in the Thai language.

A popular form of entertainment in Thailand is traditional Thai dancing. It is extremely colorful with costumes made of gold cloth and trimmed with precious gems. Intricate motions of the hands and fingers tell a story, to the accompaniment of the tinkle and tootle of Thai music.

The bustling traffic on the canals stops only long enough to make a sale, or to bargain over the price.

VIET NAM

A Divided Nation

Viet Nam is a long, narrow country liberally sprinkled with mountains, located on the east coast of the Southeast Asia land-mass.

Tourists visiting Saigon, the capital of South Viet Nam, find themselves in one of Asia's most beautiful cities. Nostalgic for their homeland, the former French rulers built Saigon in Paris' image—with magnificent wide boulevards, restful sidewalk cafes, lush green parkways bursting with flowers, great trees lining virtually all the streets.

It is a city of peaceful afternoons, for it is the custom of Saigon residents to nap from shortly after 12 o'clock until late afternoon to escape the tropical heat. During the hours of rest the shops close, traffic stops, and the city is as still as it is during the deep night hours.

Adding to the beauty of the city is the national costume worn by Vietnamese women—wide-bottomed trousers made of silk worn

39

under high-necked, long-sleeved silken tunics slit on each side. The costume provides an infinite variety of colors and patterns, although the style is always the same.

At the close of school each day the girl students ride home on bicycles, their tunics flying in the breeze. They wear wide straw hats as protection against the tropic sun.

The predominate atmosphere in modern Saigon is French because France ruled Viet Nam for almost 100 years. That rule ended in 1954 when Viet Nam was divided into two distinct nations—North Viet Nam and South Viet Nam—as a result of the Indo-China War. But the French language is still used in government and business circles, especially when Vietnamese deal with Europeans. English is also widely spoken.

Viet Nam's ancient traditions go back to China, as does so much of the history of all Southeast Asia. As far back as 250 B.C. much of what is now Viet Nam was conquered by China. Today's population of Saigon is made up partly of Chinese. In fact, Cholon, a city adjacent to Saigon with a population of more than one million, is almost entirely Chinese.

Despite the cosmopolitan flavor of its capital city, much of South Viet Nam's 66,000 square miles is rural. Most of her ten million people are peasants. The hot climate favors the farmer and as a result there is usually a rice surplus in the country.

Overall there are twenty million persons in the 127,000 square miles that make up North and South Viet Nam. Little is known, however, about what has gone on in North Viet Nam and its capital of Hanoi since the Communist government took control in 1954.

South Viet Nam, ruled by a President who is elected by the people, is a member of the United Nations. North Viet Nam is not.

Saigon is a city of wide boulevards, great trees and plush, green parkways. This view of the main portion of downtown Saigon shows it as a modern, bustling capital.

Bicycle and scooter traffic in the South Vietnamese capital is heavy. But shortly after high noon Saigon residents take a nap— on the French-style balconies of their houses or in the cool back rooms of their shops—and this street, busy with its early morning hustle and bustle, will be deserted and quiet.

At right, young boys sell balloons on a Saigon street corner in early evening hours, as a vendor of sweets awaits twilight strollers. The building in the background is the Vietnamese National Assembly building, where the nation's legislators pass the laws of the country.

42

Vietnamese writing is composed of Roman letters, like the signs in this picture, but with special marks in the form of dots and triangles to indicate the special tones of the language.

Huge wicker baskets are placed on the streets with displays of fruit and other snacks for sale to passersby. Merchants who sell the fruit carry two of the baskets at a time by the pole that connects them . . .

44

. . . as this woman does who carries her goods past an automobile parked on a Saigon street. The decorative building seen here is Saigon City Hall.

An after-supper ice cream is a treat for these three Vietnamese girls in Saigon.

A group of girl peddlers wear wide straw hats as protection against Viet Nam's tropic sun as they await customers at entrance to a shrine.

A Vietnamese youngster stands before a war horse carved onto the side of a Buddhist temple in Saigon. This particular temple is dedicated to the memory of a famous Vietnamese army hero and is also his tomb. Hence, the presence of the war horse.

Great marble urns with elaborate designs such as these are seen only in Viet Nam. Here a worshipper prays to ancestors. After her prayer she will place a joss stick, a burning piece of incense, in the urn. The sweet smell will please the gods so that they will look favorably upon her request.

The influence of China on ancient Viet Nam left Buddhism as the principal religious belief of the nation. Unlike Buddhism in other Southeast Asian nations, however, Buddhism in Viet Nam is definitely mixed with the teachings of Confucius. Here a monk prepares the altar before a large image of a stone Buddha.

This is a common sight in Saigon—college girls in their wide straw hats and long tresses walking down a tree-lined boulevard after morning classes. The white dress is the typical uniform of girl students in the capital.

This great stone serpent, a decorative sentinel at the entrance to a Saigon public building, watches as a young couple strolls through the park. The boy is dressed in western clothes, but the girl wears the national dress of Vietnamese women.

LAOS

Where Primitive Ways Remain

One of the most primitive lands in Southeast Asia is tiny Laos. Whereas the modern world is making inroads into other nations of the area, especially in the capitals, Laos is still a remote land of rugged mountains, dense forests and jungle, populated largely by tribes people.

The capital of Laos is Vientiane, a city of about 60,000 people. But it is actually only an overgrown village with a large number of yellow stucco buildings with balconies, a reminder of the days from 1893 until after World War II when France ruled the nation.

The Lao people once called their land Muong Lan Xang Hom Khao, or Land of a Million Elephants and the White Parasol.

There are no railroads in Laos and to travel from village to village you must take an airplane or drive over rugged, dusty roads through the jungle. There are only about 1,000 telephones in the whole country, and communications from village-to-village are very scarce.

In fact, the country is so primitive that the government is not sure how many people live in the 90,000 square miles of Laos. Some people say 1,500,000; others say the number is 3,000,000.

Only about half the people living in Laos are Lao. The others are Thais and mountain people who came to Laos from southern China many years ago.

The Lao—even many of those who live in Vientiane—are a superstitious people. For example, they believe there are thirty-two spirits living in their body and if they become ill it is because one of the spirits has departed. Many Lao wear a string around their wrist to keep the spirits in their body.

Like Thailand, Laos is a Buddhist nation. And, as in Thailand, the Lao call the Buddhist temples *wats*.

Early each morning Buddhist monks walk through the streets of Vientiane carrying huge bowls which women, kneeling in the street, fill with rice and other foods. This custom is also practiced in Thailand.

Almost all Lao men spend some time of their lives in a *wat* learning about Buddhism. It is common to see boys about five or six years old, their heads shaved, living and working in the *wats*.

Because of the poor communications in Laos and the lack of contact between the various tribes of the mountains and forests there has been little development. For these same reasons it will probably be a long time before modern ways come to the little kingdom.

Laos has a King but, like Thailand, political power is in the hands of a Premier. However, the Lao are very devoted to their King.

Most people who live in Laos are Buddhists. Here a bullock cart, a common means of transportation in this primitive nation, is loaded with firewood as it moves slowly past the That Luang temple, outside Vientiane. A single hair from the head of Buddha is supposed to be kept in this 400-year-old temple. Thus, it is a very holy place.

Each morning, shortly after dawn, devout Buddhist women kneel in Vientiane streets and await monks, who come begging for their breakfast. The women contribute a little to each monk and soon the priests have enough for their daily needs. This is a common sight, not only in Vientiane, but in other cities of Southeast Asia where Buddhism is the principal religion.

At left, two young Buddhist boys, members of a Vientiane *wat*, stand on the steps of their home built high on stilts. Lao houses are built like this for two reasons—to keep them dry during the monsoon season when flood waters often swirl in beneath the floors, and to provide a cool, shaded working space during the dry season.

The boys at right, studying their country's history, are reminded of great battles by an ancient war scene designed in concrete on the side of a Vientiane *wat*. Many wars have been fought in Laos because of its location in central Southeast Asia

There are not many schools in Laos outside Vientiane. This one,
built high off the ground on sturdy pillars, is one of the best in the
capital.

Two young women, shopping baskets on their arms, watch carefully before crossing Vientiane highway on their way to market. The girls wear sarongs typical of Lao women.

This handsome, young girl is a member of the Meo tribe. She can be identified by her jewelry, which is made of silver. The Meo convert much of their wealth into silver and then fashion jewelry from it.

A young boy of the Meo tribe uses a huge knife to carve a toy from a piece of wood. The Meo, distinguished by the glistening silver necklace they wear, live in the mountain country of Laos. There are many different tribes in Laos and they normally have little contact with one another.

An elderly Lao women bargains with a customer over
the price of her large wicker baskets in Vientiane market.

A group of Thais cross the dry bed of the Mekong River after the close of market in Vientiane. The river bed, which looks like an arid plain in the picture opposite, fills with water during the monsoon season. Even during the dry season there is water in the Mekong beyond the trees in the distance. On the other side of the river is Thailand.

Laos is landlocked—surrounded on all sides by other countries—and fish from the Mekong provide the people with their main supply of protein. When the waters rise to great heights, fish are easily caught with nets from shore. At this time of year the Mekong looks more like a lake than a river.

CAMBODIA

Site of Angkor Wat

Cambodia is another of Southeast Asia's primitive nations—a land of wild jungle inhabited by tigers and elephants.

The capital city, Phnom Penh, is much like Saigon in appearance, but it is not as busy as Saigon and its population is only about 500,000.

Along with Laos and Viet Nam, Cambodia was once part of France's great Indo-China colony. But because Cambodia was farther away from the Indo-China coast, she was the last of the three nations to succumb to French power.

At the end of the Indo-China War in 1954, Cambodia was made independent, entered the United Nations, and now stands as one of the area's youngest free states.

Phnom Penh still retains its French flavor, however. French is the city's second language and is used on money and postage stamps, and in business dealings with foreigners. English is seldom heard.

64

The capital city has wide boulevards, with great trees, just as Saigon does. But there are few automobiles in Phnom Penh, and the streets are unusually quiet, even at the busiest time of day. The main form of transportation is the cyclo—a small seat built on the front of a tri-cycle. A cyclo driver pedals the vehicle through the streets.

Cambodia's most famous landmark is the magnificent structure at Siem Reap called Angkor Wat. This spectacular stone temple was first built in the year 889. For 300 years the Khmer kings, as they were called, added to this temple until it became the largest religious building in the world.

Then, about 500 years ago, there was a great war at Angkor. Captives were carried away by Thai invaders and the Khmer kings moved about, finally settling at Phnom Penh. Angkor was forgotten. Tigers and elephants and snakes lived in the city. Great jungle trees grew over the magnificent temple buildings until the city was finally hidden. Just a century ago a French explorer found the lost city and today many tourists visit Angkor, considered one of the wonders of the world.

The Khmers, who ruled much of Southeast Asia for some six centuries, are gone now, but their stone monuments remain. Some of their temples are still buried in the dense jungle.

The population of Cambodia today is some five million. The nation is governed by a constitutional monarchy—that is, Cambodia has a King. But a National Assembly and a Prime Minister actually rule the country.

Cambodia is a Buddhist nation and it is a common sight to see saffron robed monks strolling the streets, under yellow umbrellas. These particular monks are on their way to the school building in the background, where they will spend the afternoon studying.

This is a typical afternoon scene in Phnom Penh, where most people nap from shortly after noon until early evening. A woman sits with a small tray of fruit for sale as a passerby scans magazines for sale. The sign in the upper portion of the picture is in Cambodian writing.

Children in America love to play with the garden hose on a hot summer afternoon—and so do these girls who are playing on the lawn of the Royal Palace in Phnom Penh. These youngsters are very fortunate because they are young dancers who will perform in costumes much like those worn by the Thai dancers shown on page 37.

This is another view of the Royal Palace. Cyclo drivers pedal their passengers down the quiet, wide thoroughfare in the Cambodian capital.

Cambodian boys find Wat Phnom, a monument to a former king of Cambodia, a fine place to play and engage in a bit of rough-house.

This boy is earning a little extra money by selling the plant he holds in his hand. The top of the plant is cut open and delicious nuts are plucked from the meat inside. The nuts are a popular afternoon snack.

This is the approach to Angkor Wat, one of Southeast Asia's most spectacular sights. For centuries this temple and city were lost in the jungle until discovered by a French explorer.

SINGAPORE
AND MALAYA

Asia's Melting Pot

Centuries ago Indian and Arab traders seeking a water route from the Indian Ocean to the South China Sea bumped into a slender strip of land now called the Malay Peninsula.

At the peninsula's southern tip was a tiny, 217-square-mile island, later called Singapore, which controlled the narrow strait that was the passageway from the Indian world to China and the Far East.

An area located so strategically between the two great giants of the Orient—China and India—could not help but become a melting pot, a curious mixture of Chinese, Indian and Moslem backgrounds.

First it was the Arabs who came in their boats. With them they brought their Islam religion, and today mosques as striking as those in Arabia await the morning and evening prayers of devout Moslems in both Singapore and Kuala Lumpur, capital of Malaya. Kuala Lumpur's skyline is typical of the Moorish cities of the Middle East.

73

After the Arabs came the Indians, and today, bearded, turbanned Sikhs are directing traffic at Kuala Lumpur's busy intersections, or standing guard in banks at Singapore.

The Indians were followed by the Western colonizers, who later imported industrious Chinese labor to develop the rich tin and rubber deposits into well-paying investments.

And this is the mixture in the Singapore-Malaya area today. Indian women in beautiful saris, Malay women in sarongs, and Chinese women in pajama-like shirt and trousers called *foo sing* rub shoulders and shop side by side in open-air markets run by Indian, Chinese and Moslem merchants. Even modern office buildings reflect the Oriental hodge-podge with their names often etched on concrete walls in three languages—English, Chinese and Sanskrit.

One of the early British colonizers in Singapore was Sir Stamford Raffles. In 1819, he decided that England should build a base on the island of Singa Pura, "The Lion City." The population was then 5,000. Like the island-city of Hong Kong, Singapore grew rapidly. Today its population is nearly two million, about 85 per cent Chinese.

England still manages Singapore's foreign affairs, although the people elect their own local government. Some day Singapore will probably be part of Malaya.

The Federation of Malayan States is a completely independent country within the British Commonwealth. It is made up of eleven states with a total area of more than 50,000 square miles. The population is some six million, about half Malay. Of the remainder about 2,500,000 are Chinese; the rest are Indians.

The states of Malaya are each headed by a man called a sultan. Although he does not have much actual power, his position reminds Malayans of the days centuries ago when each of the states was a separate country.

If you ride through the Malayan countryside you can see that it

74

is mostly wild jungle land. There are many rubber plantations and tin mines located in the jungles, however. Both these enterprises have brought a great deal of wealth to Singapore and Malaya.

Since Malaya gained independence from England in 1957 she has continued to prosper. Government officials cooperate very closely with foreign investors and many—including a large number of American firms—have invested money in factories in Malaya.

The high standard of living and prosperity have brought political stability to Malaya. Under the guidance of a Prime Minister, Malaya has taken her place well among the young nations of the United Nations.

The story of Malaya's switch from a colony of England to a free, independent state is an Asian success story of which Malayans can be proud.

A street scene in Kuala Lumpur, capital of Malaya. The man wearing the turban is a Sikh.

Kuala Lumpur has a definite Middle Eastern flavor. Its minarets and mosques, set in plush green surroundings typical of Malaya, give the city a Moorish appearance, a reminder of the days when Arab travelers came to Malaya as they sought out the wealthy Spice Islands centuries ago.

Malay women wear sarongs of many colors and designs, as do these office girls shown here as they are homeward bound from their ultra-modern, air-conditioned office building near Kuala Lumpur. Though Malay women have adopted many modern ways, they cling to their national dress.

Despite all the modern construction and up-to-date ways in 20th century Malaya, many primitive customs remain. Labor is cheap and often men and women are hired to do the work normally done by machines in most Western nations. Here an Indian woman carries rocks in a straw basket as she helps to build a parking lot.

Streamlined motor scooters zip through traffic of the capital, carrying their passengers on daily rounds. Many of the riders wear the black caps worn by Moslems in the Malay-Singapore-Indonesia area.

Modern silver trains carry commuters from the suburbs of Kuala Lumpur into the capital. Here conductors on the train check with the motorman before departure. The sign is written in Sanskrit.

Singapore, like Hong Kong, is a free port. Its stores are filled with products from all over the world, sold at moderate prices. Many different kinds of foods are available. British products are in special abundance because of Singapore's close ties with England.

Its strategic location at the tip of the Malay Peninsula has made Singapore the melting pot of Asia. Indians, Chinese and Malays shop side by side on the city's streets. The building in the background above is Sri Mariamman, Singapore's oldest Hindu temple, located in the heart of Chinatown.

Want to buy a fountain pen . . . or a balloon . . . or handker-
chiefs . . . or a toy? In the heart of Singapore everything is for sale
on makeshift counters set up along crowded sidewalks.

A typical Malay youngster sells postcards and other
tourist items in a street stall in Singapore.

A lone worshipper sits on the mat-covered floor of a great mosque in Singapore. Though Chinese make up 85 per cent of Singapore's population, there are many Moslems also. During the early morning and evening hours the mosques are crowded with the followers of Islam saying their prayers.

BURMA

Land of Buddhism

Burma is Southeast Asia's rice bowl. Thanks largely to British development of rice production during the 100 years England ruled the country, Burma now produces about 25 per cent of the world's exported rice. Much of it goes to India and Indonesia.

Virtually all of this rice is shipped through Burma's capital, Rangoon, on the Andaman Sea.

Rangoon, however, is better known throughout the world as the site of the Shwe Dagon temple, one of Buddhism's most spectacular places of worship.

Guarded by stone dogs, the Shwe Dagon is the site of a great reclining Buddha, housed at the foot of a golden pagoda which stands several stories high in the center of the temple grounds.

Buddhism is the state religion of Burma and the streets of the city are filled with robed monks attending to their duties. Many Burmese boys spend a part of their young life in the monastery learning about the religion.

The capital city itself is a bustling center of open markets, countless small shops and an ocean port visited by liners and freighters from many nations.

Rangoon's streets are colorful. A blend of Indian saris—about 30 per cent of Burma's population is Indian—with the bright sarongs and shirtwaists of Burmese women and the gaily checkered sarongs worn by Burmese men presents a constant stream of color.

Most Burmese speak their own language, but a great deal of business and official work is carried on in English, which is the country's second language. This is a reminder of the time, until 1948, when Burma was a colony of England. During World War II Japan occupied Burma, as she did virtually all of Southeast Asia. After the war Burma demanded full independence and did not join the British Commonwealth as did so many of England's former colonies.

During World War II the famous Burma Road was built over the mountains that separate Burma from China. These mountains are among the most difficult in the world to cross, but it was imperative to construct a supply line that could carry supplies to Chinese troops resisting the Japanese. The construction of the Burma Road and its role in the conflict is one of World War II's most exciting stories.

Burma, along with other young countries of Southeast Asia, has taken her seat in the United Nations. Her government is headed by a Prime Minister, elected in democratic balloting.

Rangoon is the busy capital of Burma, a sunny, tropical city of one-and-a-half million persons. This view of one of the main parts of the city shows the Sule Pagoda, a glistening golden structure. There are many pagodas in Burma, where Buddhism is the state religion.

A workman pushes his high-wheeled cart past the entrance to the Sule Pagoda in Rangoon.

The most spectacular pagoda in Rangoon is the Shwe Dagon temple, one of the most famous structures in all Southeast Asia. Here is found the great reclining Buddha of Shwe Dagon. Burmese women prepare the evening meal and exchange gossip at the foot of the Buddha.

Two worshippers arrive at the Shwe Dagon. There are many small pagodas at the temple, in addition to the main large golden dome. The writing on the pillar at the right is Burmese script, which looks a great deal like many little circles strung out one behind the other.

An old woman fingers her Buddhist beads and prays before the great temple bell at Shwe Dagon where a huge stone dog stands guard at the entrance.

During some portion of their young lives Buddhist boys spend time in a monastery studying the religion. These youngsters, their heads newly shaved, hold their saffron robes shortly after receiving them from an older monk.

Indian women, of whom there are many in Rangoon, stop at the central market to purchase food for the day's meals. Meat and vegetables are sold mainly in this central market.

Shoppers can purchase dry goods almost anywhere, however—
even on the street where this salesman has spread a cloth and
opened shop with combs, shoe polish, pens, knick-knacks and odd-
ities, all designed to catch the eye of the casual passerby. Men
wear the traditional checkered sarong worn by most Burmese
males.

One unusual market in Rangoon is the "market on the stairs"
seen opposite. All sorts of straw objects, drums, Buddhist holy
goods, and even some prepared foods are available here.

A bicycle with a side car—called a tri-shaw—is a popular form of transportation in Rangoon.

INDONESIA

Island Giant

The Republic of Indonesia is the largest and most populous nation of Southeast Asia. Made up of many islands, it is a country of great beauty and tremendous potential wealth.

Indonesia, with its capital of Jakarta, is similar to its neighbors, Malaya and Singapore, in one sense—there is an influence of the Moslem Middle East in the islands. Great white mosques built by Moslem believers, who make up about 90 per cent of the population, are common.

But there the similarity ends. Indonesia is an island nation about twice the size of Texas. The four major islands—Java, Sumatra, Borneo and Celebes—plus thousands of smaller islands, stretch 3,000 miles east and south of Malaya.

Jakarta is a city of bicycle traffic mixed with honking cars. Many Indonesians travel by *betjak*, a three-wheeled cycle pedaled by a driver in much the same fashion as the Vietnamese and Cambodian cyclos.

Running through the center of Jakarta is a wide canal in which women do the family laundry, children bathe and swim, and which the city folk generally use to cool off during the heat of the afternoons. The afternoons in Jakarta are quiet because most people nap to escape the tropical sun.

The Indonesian countryside is extremely beautiful. Conical volcanic islands rise from the ocean with symmetrical slopes that challenge the beauty of Japan's Mount Fuji. Volcanic eruptions are not uncommon and often the tranquil life of the islanders is disrupted by violent blasts. In 1883, one volcano, Mount Krakatoa, erupted with such violence that dust blown into the atmosphere by the force of the explosion was traced around the world. Some was found on the snow caps of the Arctic.

And Indonesia is an exotic country. Bali, that mystic island of the archipelago, is legendary in its beautiful dancing girls and spectacular Hindu processions.

Hinduism was Indonesia's first religion, brought to the islands by early Indian invaders. Today, Bali is virtually the only place in the archipelago that has withstood the influx of Islam which was brought to the area by Arab traders during the 13th century. Despite Moslem influence until the 16th century and the pressures of European newcomers after that, 20th century Balinese cling to their ancient Hindu beliefs and way of life.

Indonesia has potential for great wealth. With Malaya, she produces half the world's supply of tin. She is the only Southeast Asian country with important quantities of oil. Indonesian soil is rich, but food production remains low because of antiquated farming methods. Indonesia has a large working force—some ninety million persons—but over half of these people live in the 48,000 square miles of Java.

The Dutch ruled Indonesia for many years, until 1949 when independence was reluctantly granted. But the Dutch had not trained government leaders. When independence was won only

100

about 7 per cent of the people could read and write. Hence, Indonesia today faces serious problems such as increasing her production of food, establishing industrial plants in the cities, and developing the nation's natural resources.

To complicate matters, Indonesia, like many of the Southeast Asian nations that were once colonies of European powers, is wary of help from highly advanced, industrial western nations.

Indonesia is a member of the United Nations. The ruler of the country is called the President.

Indonesia's countryside is marked by terraced rice fields, like these where young shoots are just beginning to break through the thin sheet of water on the paddy. The thatched hut at the right is not a home but a rest house for the farmer to use as escape from the afternoon sun. He also lives in the hut when the rice is mature to protect it against raids by birds.

Rice is also grown in flat countryside like this. The farmer uses bullocks and a wooden plow just as his ancestors did years before him. Despite being the largest and most populous nation in Southeast Asia, Indonesian rice production is low. It is one of the serious problems the young nation faces.

Because Indonesia is always warm, young children spend a great deal of time splashing in canals and rivers to keep cool. The waterways are also used to bathe and wash.

Batik is one of Indonesia's best known exports. Here an Indonesian woman performs the painstaking process of making the beautiful material. The desired design is drawn on the cloth in wax, and then vegetable dyes are applied. The material is washed, a new design in wax applied, and the second color dye is used. After several such processes the result is a gaily colored garment of many shades and colors.

105

This is a typical market in an Indonesian town. Balloons, toys, food, household items are put out to catch the eye of passersby . . .

. . . who often come to town with baskets on their heads to be used to carry home their purchases. The mouth of this elderly woman is stained black from chewing betel nuts and tobacco.

Bali is in Indonesia, located at almost the center of the nation's many islands. It is known largely for its ancient culture and its beautiful dances. A young girl is shown here dancing to the accompaniment of drum music in front of a Hindu temple.

Another kind of dance in Bali is a tourist's treat. It is called the Barong Dance, and tells the story of an imaginary beast, the Barong, and his struggle against evil. The Barong, shown here with his friend the monkey, is colorful, with a long white mane, popping eyes and jeweled trappings. The dance is often held in the court-yard of an elaborate temple. The parts, of course, are played by actors in costume.

This man looks like he is chopping wood, but actually he is playing an Indonesian musical instrument. The mallet striking the various bars makes a sound just like a xylophone.

110

An Indonesian, wearing a hat seen often in Moslem nations of Southeast Asia, sits with his trained monkey. In some parts of the islands monkeys are trained to pick coconuts from trees. This is one such monkey with the fruit he picked.

THE PHILIPPINES

Asia's Christian Country

The Christian cathedrals of The Philippines contrast sharply with the Buddhist temples and marble mosques of other Southeast Asian countries.

It is the predominance of Christianity that sets The Philippine Islands apart from her Asian neighbors. Spanish conquerors came to the islands in the 16th century and during the 300 years of rule that followed converted the populace to Roman Catholicism.

In 1898, as a result of the Spanish-American War, the United States gained possession of the islands and began the long task of preparing the Filipinos for independence.

Thus, the modern-day Philippines, and especially the capital city of Manila, are a colorful mixture of Spanish and American influences.

Many people speak English in the islands, but with a heavy Spanish accent. Menfolk prefer American styles, but women often wear veils of beautiful lace exactly like their counterparts in

112

Madrid. The national dress of Filipino women is also decidedly Spanish in style.

Sweeping boulevards in Manila carry traffic into the heart of the city where high-wheeled Spanish *calisas* drawn by ponies compete with jeepneys—enlarged U. S. Army jeeps—for the taxi trade.

The Escolta—one of Manila's important shopping areas—could be almost any American main street despite its Spanish name.

The Filipinos themselves are a fun-loving people. They have often been called the Latins of the Orient because of their natural gift for music and their gracious personalities.

For many Americans the names of Philippine islands and cities bring memories of World War II—Mindanao, Luzon, Corregidor, Bataan. Thousands of Americans died defending these islands against Japanese attack and invasion. And thousands more died winning them back. In Manila today there is a cemetery where many of the American soldiers who were killed in the fighting are buried.

America's benevolent rule of the islands and the American-Filipino comradeship during World War II have developed strong ties between the two countries. They often stand side by side in the United Nations and both are members of the Southeast Asia Treaty Organization.

A government much like that of the United States rules the 7,000 islands of The Philippines. A President is elected by the people and legislative bodies enact the laws.

This is Manila, capital of The Philippines. It is a city of wide boulevards like this one and big government office buildings. This scene is similar to that in many American cities.

But the capital has narrow streets, too, crowded with pony-drawn *calisas* that are used as taxis by many of the people who live in The Philippines. Like all Southeast Asian cities, Manila has a Chinatown. *Calisas* are especially abundant in this section of the city.

A popular form of motorized transportation is the jeepney—an old American Army jeep with an enlarged body, gaily decorated and built to carry ten or more passengers.

Coat hangers, soap and numerous other household items are sold from makeshift stands on Manila's streets.

When Manila first became an important Spanish city, the rulers built a sturdy stone wall to fortify it. The wall still stands and today this section of the city is called "The Walled City." Many poor families make their homes in the tunnels of the old wall. They make an entrance out of scraps of lumber, as the family seen opposite has done.

Two school girls of the Philippines.

This is Santa Thomas University, one of Southeast Asia's oldest universities, located in Manila.

The influence of Christianity is strong in The Philippines. Roman Catholic cathedrals, such as this one, are found in Manila. More than 90 per cent of the country's population is Catholic.

Despite the modern atmosphere of Manila, most of the people in the nation's 7,000 islands live in *barrios*, or small villages. This little boy rides a huge water buffalo. He lives about fifty miles from the capital, and is on his way to meet friends.

Cock fighting is a favorite sport of the Filipinos. Raising birds that are good fighters is considered an art. Oftentimes the spectators bet money on the outcome of the cock fight.

Thousands of American soldiers who died defending the islands from Japanese attack during World War II are buried in the Manila American Cemetery and Memorial. The cemetery was constructed by the United States as a resting place for American soldiers who gave their lives in this battle area.

Index

About the Author-Photographer

Hal Buell, the author-photographer of MAIN STREETS OF SOUTH-EAST ASIA, lives in Tokyo, Japan, where he is assigned as Asian Photo Editor of the Associated Press.

He has lived in Japan for three years with his wife, Angela, a teacher, and his six-year-old daughter, Barbara. He was also assigned to Japan as a cameraman while serving in the U. S. Army.

A Chicagoan by birth, Buell is 31 and a graduate of Northwestern University. MAIN STREETS OF SOUTHEAST ASIA is his second photographic book for youngsters. His first, YOUNG JAPAN, was about the children of the country in which he now lives.

Hal Buell has spent five years working in Asia and has traveled widely in the area between Japan and India. He is well-acquainted with Southeast Asia and his excellent photographs present a fascinating and dramatic portrait of this particular corner of the world.